And Still They Bloom

And Still They Bloom

A Family's Journey of Loss and Healing

Written by Amy Rovere

Illustrated by Joel Spector

Published by the American Cancer Society
Health Promotions
250 Williams Street NW
Atlanta, Georgia 30303 USA

Manufactured by Dickinson Press, Inc.
Manufactured in Grand Rapids, MI, in May 2012
Job # 4019500

Printed in the United States of America
Design by Krystyna Skalski; composition by Bernadette Evangelist Design, New York, NY
5 4 3 2 1   12 13 14 15 16

Library of Congress Cataloging-in-Publication Data
Rovere, Amy.
And still they bloom: a family's journey of loss and healing / written by Amy Rovere; illustrated by Joel Spector.
    p. cm.
  ISBN 978-1-60443-036-3 (hardcover: alk. paper) — ISBN 1-60443-036-2 (hardcover: alk. paper)
  I. Spector, Joel. II. Title.
PZ7.R783An 2013
[E] — dc23

                                    2012006637

American Cancer Society
Managing Director, Content: Chuck Westbrook
Director, Cancer Information: Terri Ades, DNP, FNP-BC, AOCN
Director, Book Publishing: Len Boswell
Managing Editor, Book Publishing: Rebecca Teaff, MA
Senior Editor, Book Publishing: Jill Russell
Book Publishing Coordinator: Vanika Jordan, MSPub
Editorial Assistant, Book Publishing: Amy Rovere

For more information about cancer, contact your American Cancer Society at **800-227-2345** or **cancer.org**.

Quantity discounts on bulk purchases of this book are available. For information, please contact the American Cancer Society, Health Promotions Publishing, 250 Williams Street NW, Atlanta, GA 30303-1002, or send an e-mail to **trade.sales@cancer.org**.

In memory of Judith,
and to Isabella with all my love

EMILY sat down on the back porch steps and took a deep breath. She wrapped her arms around her knees and gently rocked back and forth. She felt relieved to be alone. It was almost warm, unusual for early spring. It was Emily's tenth birthday. Looking out at the garden, her mother's garden, she noticed some signs of life starting to break through the damp earth. Emily hadn't spent much time in the backyard—not since her mother had gotten sick. She hadn't noticed until now that the bulbs they planted together were starting to poke up and out of the ground. Tears streamed down Emily's cheeks as she realized that her mother would never see them bloom.

Emily quickly wiped away her tears when she heard the screen door open and shut with a bang. Her seven-year-old brother, Ben, came bounding onto the porch. "Are you ready to play with me?" he asked as he sat down beside her. "I want to try your new game."

"Go away, Ben. I want to be alone," she said quietly.

"But you said you'd play with me after the party," he whined.

"I said, GO AWAY!" Emily shouted as she hugged her knees even tighter. Ben didn't move. He just sat there sulking, which made her even angrier.

The screen door opened again, and the floorboards creaked as their father crossed the porch. Emily waited for him to speak, but he was silent as he sat down beside them on the steps. They sat together quietly looking out at the garden.

Her father was the first to break the silence. "I'm sorry she wasn't here to help us celebrate, Emily. But I'm glad that Grace and Anna could come to the party."

"I don't feel much like celebrating." Emily looked down at her feet. She was quiet for a moment. "I just don't understand. Why did Mom have to die? It's not fair!"

Her father placed his hand in hers. "I know it's not fair, Emily. I wish Mom was here, too." He paused briefly. "Life's not always fair. Some people can have cancer, get better, and live a very long life. Other people get so sick that they die."

Emily noticed a few tears start to form in his eyes. "But why doesn't everyone get better? Sarah's mom had cancer, but she didn't die. Her mom still makes her favorite foods, and drives her to dance class, and tucks her into bed at night."

"That's not an easy question to answer, Em. As hard as they try, sometimes the doctors can't make cancer go away."

"And that's what happened to Mom?" Ben asked. "Her cancer wouldn't go away?"

He answered softly, "Yes."

Emily was quiet, debating whether to ask her next question. She wasn't sure that she really wanted to know the answer. Before she could make up her mind, Ben beat her to it.

"What if you get cancer?" he asked.

"I know you're both worried that you could lose me, too," their father said gently. "But I'm healthy. And I'll do my best to stay well, so we can be together for a long time. If I ever get sick, the doctors will do everything possible to help me get well. Aunt Paula and Uncle Neil would take care of you if I couldn't. I know you're both scared, but just because Mom died doesn't mean the same thing will happen with me."

Ben looked relieved. More than anything, Emily wanted to believe what her father had said was true, but she wasn't so sure. The sun hung low in the sky and cast shadows across the yard. They sat together on the steps for a long time.

❊ ❊ ❊

A FEW WEEKS later, Emily and Ben were putting the groceries away after a trip to the store. As Ben reached for the box of his favorite snacks, Emily snatched them out of his hands.

"Back off, squirt," she declared. "These are mine."

"No fair!" Ben shouted, as he tried to grab the box.

"Quit it, you two!" their father piped in. "There's enough for everybody."

Emily threw the box on the floor and sat down on a stool next to the counter. She knew her father would be mad but she didn't care. She was angry and annoyed, and it didn't matter if he scolded her.

At the grocery store, they had run into some women from her mother's garden club. Emily had felt awkward standing there waiting for her father to finish being polite so they could leave. She had grown to hate these moments. She knew people meant well when they said things like, "She's in a better place now," or "At least she's at peace." But these words were not comforting to Emily. And when she heard them she wanted to scream! There was no better place for her mother than home. Nothing anyone could say would make her believe anything else. No one could make her pain go away. People could say all kinds of things, but what was the point? She wished they'd all just go away and leave them alone.

Her father reached down and picked up the box of snacks. He took out two small pouches, tossed one to Ben, and handed one to Emily. "Hey, Ben," her father began. "Can you give me and your sister some time to talk? Why don't you go play in your room, and I'll come talk to you in a few minutes."

"Why do people say those things?" Emily shouted angrily after Ben had left the room. "Mom's not at peace. She's dead, and she's never coming back! They make it sound like she's happier now that she's away from us. Why would they say something so mean? Did Mom want to die? Did she want to leave us behind?"

Her father answered. "I know you're angry, Emily. You've got a lot to be angry about. No, Mom didn't want to die. She wanted more than anything to be here with us right now." He pulled a stool up next to her and sat down.

"Those women today meant well. They're sad about Mom, too. She was their friend, and they're just trying to say something nice. People deal with sadness in different ways. Sometimes people say those things because it makes them feel better. Many people loved Mom and miss her a lot. It's hard to know the right thing to say to someone who feels sad, and people just do the best they can."

"Some kids at school don't say anything at all to me. They just look at me funny or whisper when I walk by," Emily admitted. "At least Anna and Grace are still my friends. They still play with me."

"I'm sorry that some kids have acted that way, Emily. That must be really hard for you. I'm sure those kids feel sad about Mom, too. They might also feel embarrassed because they want to help but don't always know what to say. Often, when people don't know what to say, they don't say anything at all. I know that can be hurtful. Some kids also might be scared and confused. They might worry that what happened to Mom will happen to someone they love. I hope that with time, the other kids will follow Anna's and Grace's example and not treat you any differently."

Emily hung her head down, unable to meet her father's eyes. In

a whisper, she said, "Sometimes I'm so angry at her for leaving us. Does that make me a bad person?"

Her father brushed back a stray piece of hair that had fallen in her eyes. "You're not a bad person for feeling angry. It's very hard to lose someone you love. It's okay to feel sad and scared, and even angry, too. We have so many feelings inside of us. They're all okay. Talking about it can help you feel better. I'm always here to listen. Don't be afraid to tell me how you feel."

Emily hugged her father, and the warmth of his arms comforted her. She felt so many things, and her feelings were all jumbled up inside her. It was hard to know how to sort them all out. But now, she just felt tired and didn't want to talk anymore. She rested her head on his chest. "I love you, Emily," he said. "We'll get through this together."

❊ ❊ ❊

BEN had wrapped himself tightly in his favorite blanket, the one his mother had made. He was sitting on the floor next to his bed when he heard a knock on the door. His father stepped into the room and joined Ben on the floor.

"Hey buddy," his father said quietly.

Ben clutched his blanket even tighter and scowled.

"You want to talk about it?" his father asked.

Ben nodded. "Why is Emily so mean to me? She's mad all the time and doesn't want to play with me." As a single tear ran down his cheek, he whispered, "Did I do something wrong? Was it my fault that Mom died? Is that why Emily's so mad at me?"

His father put his arm around Ben and said, "No, Ben. It's no one's fault—not yours, not mine, not Emily's."

Ben didn't realize he'd been holding his breath waiting for an answer. He breathed out, and soon his cheeks were wet with tears.

His father paused, searching for the right words. "Sometimes, people get sick. Most of the time, they get better. But, in some cases, no matter what anyone does to help, they still die." He continued, "Emily is not mad at you, Ben. She's angry and upset that Mom died. Sometimes when people are hurting, they take it out on those around them—even the people they love."

Ben sucked in his breath to try to stop crying as he wiped his wet face. He listened as his father continued.

"We're all upset that Mom died, though sometimes we have different ways of showing it. The important thing, Ben, is to let your feelings out and not keep them inside."

He looked directly at Ben. "It's okay to cry when sad things happen."

"Even for boys?" Ben asked.

"Even for boys," his father said with certainty. "Even I cry sometimes. It's much better to let your feelings out than to keep them locked up inside. You can always talk to me about how you feel. Nana and Papa, too. We're always here for you."

His father held Ben close before he stood up and said, "I'll be right back; I have something for you."

He was only gone a moment before he returned with a cloth bag. He sat back down on the floor. He reached inside the bag and retrieved a small narrow box and handed it to Ben.

The leather box was smooth to the touch. As his father opened it, Ben recognized the slender, shiny object inside. It was his mother's fountain pen. Ben picked up the pen; it felt cool in his hand.

"It's Mom's special pen," Ben said.

"That's right. She'd use it to write down all her thoughts and feelings when she was happy or sad. I brought you a notebook, too, just like the one she used. You can draw pictures or write down your feelings whenever you want."

Ben opened the notebook and ran his fingers along the crisp white pages. He pictured his mother at her small writing desk in front of the window. He remembered how the sunlight would make her hair shine. She was so pretty. He closed his hand tightly around the pen. Ben thanked his father and clutched him hard around the middle.

"Why can't she come back?" Ben asked as he buried his face into his father's chest.

"I wish she could, Ben. But that's not the way life works. Sometimes we don't have as much time as we'd like with the people we love," he said as he hugged Ben tighter.

Ben was quiet, not knowing what to say.

After a moment, his father said, "I'm going to start dinner. Want to help?"

Ben shook his head, and his father slowly got to his feet. "I'm making mac and cheese—your favorite."

"Thanks, Dad." Ben said. He looked at the notebook, wondering what to write.

❀ ❀ ❀

A LITTLE while later, Emily gently knocked on the door to her brother's room. When she opened it a crack, she could see him curled up on his bed clutching his blanket and looking at the notebook. He had been crying.

"What do you want?" he sniffled.

"I'm sorry, Ben," Emily said as she sat on the bed next to her brother. "I feel so angry at times, but I'm not mad at you. I'm sorry I took it out on you today."

Ben sat up and wiped his nose on his sleeve. "You're not the only one, Emily!"

Emily rested her hand on her brother's shoulder and tried to comfort him.

"I think about Mom all the time," he said. "I want her to come back."

"Me too, Ben, but, it's just you and me and Dad from now on. We'll be okay—you'll see." Emily tried to sound convincing for Ben's sake, but she wasn't sure she really believed it.

"Want to play the game I got for my birthday?" she asked. "You beat me the last time, and I want a rematch."

"Okay," he said. "But only if I get to be the blue guy this time."

"Only if you get there first!" she shouted as she started toward the door. She paused for a moment, giving him a chance to leap from the bed and out the door ahead of her.

❀ ❀ ❀

LATER in her room, Emily sat on her bed and listened to the heavy spring rain pouring down. She thought about her mother as she looked at the small wooden box beside her. She remembered the times they'd played with the shiny necklaces and sparkling earrings tucked away in the tiny drawers of her mother's jewelry box. Emily picked up one simple strand of pearly white beads. On special occasions, her mother would let her wear this necklace. Although it was not made of real pearls, it was special because it had been hand beaded by her mother. Emily had felt such pride when wearing her mother's favorite

necklace. Now when she looked at it, she only wanted to cry. She carefully put the necklace away in the top drawer of the jewelry box. She was wiping the tears from her eyes when she heard a knock at the door.

"Come in," she said softly.

As he entered her room, her father could see her red eyes and tear-stained cheeks. "You okay, Em? Do you want to talk?" he asked.

Emily nodded. "I miss her so much."

He sat down on the bed and gave her a tender, bittersweet smile. "I know you do, sweetie. I really miss Mom, too."

"I can't believe she's really gone. How can we live without her, Dad?" Emily cried.

"One day at a time, Emily. I know it's hard to believe that it's possible to live without Mom. You and Ben might feel lost right now. Sometimes I feel that way, too—like I'm out in the ocean, barely managing to keep my head above the water and trying to find steady ground. But sweetheart, it's within our reach. It may take some time, but we'll get there. And as long as we've got each other—you, me, and Ben—we're not alone. And remember, Mom will always be with us."

"I don't understand," Emily said through her tears.

"Mom will always be with you—in your heart, your mind, and your spirit. She's a part of you, and nothing can ever change

that. You carry her with you wherever you go. Mom loved you so very much. Her love will stay with you always."

Emily looked at her father, and he saw the pain and sadness in her wide round eyes. "Will I always feel this way? Will it always hurt so much?"

He paused and said, "I know you're hurting; I'm hurting, too. I know it might be hard to understand this right now, Emily, but it will get easier over time. We'll always miss Mom, and some days you will feel more sad than others. Your grief will come and go, but you won't always feel this way."

Emily had a hard time believing that the pain inside her would ever go away. How could it if her mother was never coming back? She looked out the window. Who would take care of her mother's garden now that she was gone? How would the plants survive if her mother wasn't there to take care of them? How would she?

❊ ❊ ❊

ONE NIGHT, Ben couldn't sleep and wandered downstairs. He found his father sitting alone in the living room holding a golden picture frame. There were tears in his eyes.

Seeing Ben, his father put the picture down on the table beside the couch. "Can't sleep, buddy?" he asked.

Ben climbed up on the couch beside his father and shook his head.

"Are you okay, Dad?" Ben asked.

"I'm just sad. Everything reminds me of Mom," his father said as he looked at her picture on the table.

"You can borrow Mom's pen anytime you want," Ben said as he looked up at his father. "It makes me feel better when I use it."

His father smiled tenderly and pulled Ben closer to him. "Thanks, bud."

"Will you sing to me?" Ben asked. "The way she did?"

They snuggled up together on the couch. As his father softly sang, Ben fell asleep in his arms.

❋ ❋ ❋

ONE SUNDAY afternoon, Emily relaxed on the porch swing while she watched her father and brother out in the yard. Their father dipped a large wand in a shallow pan of suds and waved it slowly through the air, making large soap bubbles. Emily liked to watch the beautiful bubbles gently float in the breeze. The sunlight made colorful rings on the edges of the bubbles. Emily wished that she could stop time and make them last forever.

"Emily, look. Aren't these the flowers you and Mom planted

together?" her father asked from across the yard.

Emily sat up and spotted her father pointing to a large patch of green earth. Tall shoots were poking through the ground. She walked out into the yard and stood next to her father. As she looked down, she wondered how much longer it would be before the bright yellow blossoms appeared at the top of the dark green stalks. It didn't really matter, she decided, since her mom wouldn't be there to see them bloom.

"Why does everything have to change?" Emily asked.

"Change is part of life, sweetheart. And you can see it all around you in the garden. Life's always changing. Some things will be very different now, and many things will stay the same. We'll still do many of the things we did when Mom was with us, and we'll do them together. I may not do things exactly how she did, but I'll try my best."

Her father smiled a bit. "We can try new things together, too, like keeping up Mom's garden. She loved working outside, and being out here makes me feel closer to her." He paused. "We can help each other remember the good times we had as a family while we're making new memories together."

Ben came running up to them from across the yard. "Did you see, Emily? Did you see? Mom's Daffy Dills are almost here!"

"Yes, I see the Daffy Dills." Emily smiled and remembered her mother calling them just that. She turned to Ben and asked,

"How about some more bubbles?"

"Yes!" screamed Ben.

Ben handed her a wand and together they filled the yard with more bubbles than they could count. They took turns trying to catch each bubble before it popped.

❋ ❋ ❋

EMILY AND BEN spent many afternoons in the sunroom facing the garden. One day, Emily curled up with her sketchbook and colored pencils while Ben sat beside her with his notebook in his lap. Through the window, they could see their father as he pulled weeds outside. Lately, he had been spending a lot of time out in the garden.

Sunlight fell on an open photo album on the nearby coffee table. Emily looked longingly at the pictures from a family trip to Hunting Island last summer. She gazed at a picture of herself with her mother and Ben, all striking silly poses on the sandy beach. Their mother had said something to make them laugh, right before that picture was taken. Only now, neither could remember what she had said. How Emily wished she could remember! Would she ever feel that happy again? She was so lost in the memory that she didn't notice the phone ringing. A few minutes later, her father's footsteps echoed as he came down the hall. She put down her sketchbook as he entered the room.

"Emily, Anna called and wants to know if you'll be coming to her sleepover. She hopes you can make it."

Emily answered, "I really don't feel like going, Dad. Anna will understand."

"The choice is yours, sweetie. But you always have so much fun together. Are you sure you don't want to change your mind?"

"Wouldn't it be wrong for me to go and have fun — like nothing has happened? How can I ever be happy again with Mom gone?" Emily asked.

"Mom wouldn't want you to be sad all the time. She would want you to play and have fun with your friends. You can miss her but still feel happy sometimes, too."

Emily hung her head, not sure she understood what he meant. She found it hard to believe she could ever feel happy again.

"The daffodils are blooming. I guess spring's arrived," he said as he placed a vase of bright yellow blossoms on the table. "What are you guys working on?" he asked.

"We're drawing pictures of Mom." Emily looked down at her sketchbook. "Well, I tried to draw Mom, but I had to look at her picture. When I try to see her in my mind, it's like she's fading away. Ben feels the same." She glanced at Ben. "We don't ever want to forget her, Dad."

"Remember when I told you that Mom will always be with us?" their father reminded them. "Her memory will continue to live

on in the hearts and minds of everyone who loved her. We can remember the good times we spent together and look at pictures if we need reminding." Looking at the photo album, he smiled. "You know, guys, there are lots of things we can do together to honor her memory. Drawing pictures is one of them; keeping up Mom's garden is another."

Her father reached out and picked up Emily's sketchbook. "Did you know that you and Mom have the same smile?" he said to her. Then he looked at Ben. "All I have to do is look at both of you to feel close to her." Ben smiled as his father handed the sketchbook back to Emily. He tousled Ben's hair and kissed the top of Emily's head before leaving the room. Emily thought for a moment about what her father had said. She liked the part about having her Mom with her always, even though her heart still ached and she didn't feel like smiling.

❄ ❄ ❄

WEEKS passed and spring turned into summer. Emily and Ben began to spend more time with their father in the garden. Some days, Emily would sketch while Ben pulled weeds and their father trimmed bushes. Some days, she would help plant new seeds or watch as others took root and bloomed. Vibrant colors and lush green stalks appeared all over the yard.

Anna and Grace would often come over to play, and the children would have adventures out in the garden. They helped Emily

and Ben collect pieces of broken tile, and together they made a colorful stone path. At the end of the path was a small wooden bench surrounded by bright pink azaleas. Many days, Emily would sit and sketch or just observe the changes all around her. Ben would fill page after page in his notebook. On other days, they would leap from stone to stone chasing after butterflies. At these moments, Emily and Ben could forget, if only for a brief time, that their mother was gone.

Just as their father had predicted, their grief would come and go like waves—first crashing down hard and leaving them breathless, then slowly fading only to come back again. Many days, they still felt lost and empty inside. Sometimes, Emily imagined that she would wake up from this terrible dream and her mother would be right there with her. During those times, she found comfort getting lost in her favorite book, sitting on the porch swing, drawing in her sketchbook, or playing with Ben. Gradually, she learned to be open to moments of joy wherever she could find them. Emily realized that happiness was not going to be a constant feeling, but it could be found in little moments that came about when you least expected them. Ben let his feelings pour out on the pages of his notebook, and each time he wrote, he seemed to hurt just a little bit less. Slowly, they both adjusted to life's different rhythm.

❋ ❋ ❋

SOON SUMMER would be over, and Emily and Ben would return to school. They spent the last of the long summer nights in the garden. One evening Emily looked around and realized just how much the garden had changed since early spring. Across the yard, Ben looked taller, too. Her father's words echoed in her head: "Change is a part of life." Emily wondered what school would be like this year. Would she still be "the girl whose mom had died"? She had started to worry about other things, too, like how their lives might change in other ways.

Later that night, Emily was surprised by the question her brother suddenly asked in the middle of dinner.

"Dad, do you think you'll ever get married again?" Ben asked.

Emily made swirls in her mashed potatoes and stared at her plate. Her father put down his fork and waited to speak until Emily lifted her head. "No one can ever replace Mom. She was an amazing woman and a wonderful mother, and I will always love her. There's no one in the whole world like her."

He waited for his words to sink in and took a deep breath. "Ben, I don't know whether I'll ever get married again. But, even if I do, I want you both to know that I'll *always* love you. Being your dad is the most important thing in the world to me, and nothing and no one will ever change that."

As Emily listened to her father, she touched the necklace clasped around her neck. She had begun to wear her mother's pearls more often, and not just on special occasions. At first,

wearing them made her feel sad. Slowly, though, she had begun to find comfort in the things she and her mother had shared.

"That necklace looks beautiful on you, sweetheart," her father said. "I'm glad to see that you have started to wear it again." Emily blushed at her father's compliment. Until then, she wasn't sure the emptiness inside her would ever go away. But in that moment, she felt pride in wearing the necklace. It was a reminder of her mother, who would always be in her heart. They shared a bond that could never be broken.

❄ ❄ ❄

LATER, as Emily stood on the porch looking out at the garden, she was amazed by the bold changes in the world around her. The daffodil blooms were long gone, but the memory of their bright yellow blossoms stayed with her. The garden had changed, and so had her family. She knew her mother would have been proud of them. It had taken time, but they had found their steady ground. Whatever the future held, they would face it together.

The back door opened and Ben bounded down the steps into the yard. "Bet you can't catch me!" he shouted.

"Bet I can!" Emily called as she ran after him. As the sun slowly set behind the trees, their laughter echoed through the garden.

Acknowledgments

I WANT TO THANK my family for their endless support and encouragement: my best friend and husband, Ricky, and my daughter, Isabella, who have been a tremendous source of inspiration. I would also like to thank Jon and Pam Rovere, Dan Rovere, Doris and Morton Fleischer, and Helen Hornstein for accompanying me on this journey. My sincere thanks to the following people for their numerous contributions: Chuck Westbrook, Len Boswell, Rebecca Teaff, Jill Russell, Vanika Jordan, Donna Schuurman, Silvia Strauss, and Heather Sorensen. Without them, this book would not be possible.

About the Author

AMY ROVERE is a writer, editor, and artist. Originally from Longmeadow, Massachusetts, Amy studied theatrical design in Baltimore, Maryland, and worked in publishing and the arts until relocating to Decatur, Georgia, in 2000. In her work at the American Cancer Society, she helps create books for patients and families who are coping with cancer.

When she was just nine years old, Amy lost her mother to cancer. *And Still They Bloom* was inspired by this loss and by her desire to help children going through a similar experience. Amy is a member of the American Medical Writers Association, the Society for Children's Book Writers and Illustrators, and the Atlanta Collage Society. She lives in Decatur with her husband, Ricky, and daughter, Isabella.

About the Illustrator

JOEL SPECTOR was born in Havana, Cuba, and came to the United States at age twelve. He graduated from the Fashion Institute of Technology and received a Master of Fine Arts degree from Western Connecticut State University. Joel began his career in fashion illustration and later moved to general illustration, specializing in portraiture.

Among other numerous awards, Joel was recently named winner of the 2011 International Portrait Competition and the Artist's Magazine 2011 Competition. His work has appeared in many print publications and has been shown at the New Britain Museum of American Art, the Slater Memorial Museum, and various galleries. Joel lives in New Milford, Connecticut, with his wife, Rowena, and their four children, Max, Ari, Jacob, and Saskia.

Resources

American Cancer Society
250 Williams Street, 6th Floor
Atlanta, GA 30303-1002
Toll-free: 800-227-2345
Internet: www.cancer.org

The American Cancer Society is the nationwide community-based, voluntary health organization dedicated to eliminating cancer as a major health problem by preventing cancer, saving lives, and diminishing suffering from cancer through research, education, advocacy, and service. Headquartered in Atlanta, Georgia, the Society has state divisions and more than 3,400 local offices. The American Cancer Society provides educational materials, information, and patient services. A comprehensive resource for all your cancer-related questions, the Society can also put you in touch with community resources in your area.

National Alliance for Grieving Children
555 Forest Avenue
Portland, ME 04101-1504
Toll-free: 866-432-1542
Email: info@nationalallianceforgrievingchildren.org
Internet: www.nationalallianceforgrievingchildren.org

The National Alliance for Grieving Children provides a network for nationwide communication between hundreds of children's bereavement centers who want to share ideas, information, and resources with each other to better support the families they serve in their own communities.

The Centering Corporation
7230 Maple Street
Omaha, NE 68134
Toll-free: 866-218-0101
Fax: 402-553-0507
Internet: www.centering.org

The Centering Corporation is a non-profit organization dedicated to providing education and resources for the bereaved. They publish books for children and adults and provide educational offerings and workshops for caregivers and families.

The Association for Death Education and Counseling
111 Deer Lake Road, Suite 100
Deerfield, IL 60015
Telephone: 847-509-0403
Fax: 847-480-9282
Internet: www.adc.org

The Association for Death Education and Counseling is one of the oldest interdisciplinary organizations in the field of dying, death, and bereavement. Its nearly 2,000 members include a wide array of mental and medical health personnel, educators, clergy, funeral directors, and volunteers.

Other Books for Children Published by the American Cancer Society

Available everywhere books are sold and online at **cancer.org/bookstore**

Because… Someone I Love Has Cancer

Get Better! Communication Cards for Kids & Adults

Healthy Me: A Read-Along Coloring & Activity Book

Imagine What's Possible: Using the Power of Your Mind to Take Control of Your Life During Cancer

Kids' First Cookbook: Delicious-Nutritious Treats to Make Yourself!

Let My Colors Out

The Long and the Short of It: A Tale About Hair

Mom and the Polka-Dot Boo-Boo

Nana, What's Cancer?

No Thanks, but I'd Love to Dance: Choosing to Live Smoke Free

Our Dad Is Getting Better

Our Mom Has Cancer (available in hard cover and paperback)

Our Mom Is Getting Better

The Survivorship Net: A Parable for the Family, Friends, and Caregivers of People with Cancer

What's Up with Bridget's Mom? Medikidz Explain Breast Cancer

What's Up with Jo? Medikidz Explain Brain Tumors

What's Up with Lyndon? Medikidz Explain Osteosarcoma

What's Up with Richard? Medikidz Explain Leukemia

What's Up with Tiffany's Dad? Medikidz Explain Melanoma

Visit **cancer.org/bookstore** for a full listing of books published by the American Cancer Society.